COMBO OF IMO AND IGCSE GRADE 5

SURYA PRATAP SINGH

Contents

CHAPTER ONE

COUNTING ON BACK IN FRACTIONS AND DECIMALS

Count on or back in the steps given

Count on in steps of 0.2

3.5 -.-,-,4.3,--,---,-- 4.9,----,----

Count back in steps of 0.01

6.22,----,-----,------ , 6.18,-----,----,6.15,----,------

Count back in steps of 1/2

8 1/2 ,------,-----,---- 6 1/2 ,----,-----,5,-----,------

Count on or back in the steps given

a. Count on in steps of 0.4

7.7 ,-----,------,-----

b. Count back in steps of 0.03

5.55 ,------,---------,--------

c. Count on in steps of 0.05

3.114 ,-------,-------,------ 2.214,------,-----

Count forwards in steps of 0.05 from 2.11

2.16 2.19 2.22 2.27 2.3 2.34 2.39

2.43 , 2.48, 2.53

Count forwards in 0.6s from 4.6

2nd term -------- 4th term 5th term

CHAPTER TWO

FINDING TERMS OF A SQUARE NUMBER SEQUENCE

1x1 = 1

2x2 = 4

A square number is a result when a number has been multiplied by itself

Position Calculation Value

1

2

3

4

5

6

7

8

9

10

Answer the following questions

Find the area of a rectangle whose length = 15 cm breadth = 16 cm

The children in a assembly arrange themselves in 8 rows of 8 How many children are there

The flowers are arranged in 7 rows of 7 How many flowers are there

The beds are arranged in 13 rows of 13 How many beds are there

CHAPTER THREE

Number Sense

1. Write Eighty million Sixty thousand sixty in numeral form

2.Largest 5 digit number that can be formed by using digits 5,3,0,8 each atleast once

3.Shikha makes a profit of rupees thirty five crofit ore four lakh thirty five thousand fifty nine Write the profit in the Indian System

4. What will we get if we add 1 to the smallest 7 digit number

5.Round off the number 46579 to nearest hundreds

6 How many four digit numbers can be formed by using 8,5,0,8 only once in a number

7. The greatest four digit number that can be formed using digits of Gopal car number 2887 will have at its tens place

8. Identify the number using given clues

I am an odd number

My tens digit is greatest one digit number

My hundreds digit is even number

My thousands digit is the latest odd number

9. The difference between the place value of 9 and 5 in 68905

10. 68234 is 68230 when rounded off to the nearest ----------

CHAPTER FOUR

ADDING POSITIVE AND NEGATIVE NUMBERS

Add

- 4 + 2 -7 +5

-6 + 1 -7 + 17

-8 + 5 -1 + 8

-7 + 4

-10 + 9

-2 + 8

Use the number line to find the sum

-11 + 8

-14 + 13

- 12 + 5

-17 + 12

-18 + 13

-19 + 15

-22 + 19

- 21 + 12

-25 + 17

Calculate the new bank balance Write the calculation

Starting balance Money in New Balance Calculation

-16 32

-18 62

-11 42

-14 23

-4 53

-2 37

Write two numbers a negative augend and a positive addenda that will give each total

------ + -------- =-5

------ +--------- = -7

-------+ --------- =-1

------- + --------- = -6

CHAPTER FIVE

ADDING POSITIVE AND NEGATIVE NUMBERS (2)

a. What is 7 degrees more than -14 degree C

b. What is 9 degrees more than - 40 degree C

c. What is 12 degrees more than - 8 degree C

d. What is 15 degrees more than - 6 degree C

e . What is 25 degrees more than -14 degree C

f. What is 8 degrees more than - 17 degree C

g. What is 3 degrees more than -13 degreee C

h What is 4 degrees more than - 16 degree C

i What is 5 degrees more than - 12 degrees C

j What is 3 degrees more than - 11 degrees C

k. What is 4 degrees more than -15 degrees C

CHAPTER SIX

IDENTIFYING VALUES FOR SYMBOLS IN SUBTRACTION CALCULATIONS

Work out the unknown values

1. 64-a = 32 a=
2. c-19=43 c=
3. b-27 =24 b =
4. 56-d =17 d =
5, 23-g = 18 g =
6 24 -h = 17 h=
7. 45-j = 95 j=
8 24-k = 46 k=
9 14- l = 55 l=
10 17-m =44 m =
11 22-U = 22 U =
12 23-V = 23 V =
13 34-W = 21 W=
14 23-X = 25 X=
15 24- B = 24 B=
16 27-C = 24 C

8

CHAPTER SEVEN

COMPUTATION OPERATIONS

1. A factory produced 800732 chips in June month Out of these 5478 chips were found of bad quality.How many chips were of good quality

'2 A factory produced 486812 Natraj pencils and 551653 pens of another kind All the pencils are mixed thouroughly and packed equally in 296 boxes How many pencils are packed in a box

3 Which of the following number is prime

a. 35

b. 66

c. 17

d. 56

4* twice the difference between the 5 th and 15 th multiple of 8 . Find *

5 What must be subtracted from 2 million to get 999600

6 The number of prime factors of 40 are

7 The product of 214 and a number is Y. Taking 39 away from X gives 1339

Find the number

8 Subtract the sum of 65236535 and 1124364 from 51276343

9 The quotient when 22415 is divided by 5

10 Farmer Shyam packed an equal number of apples into each of the 20 packets If each packet contain

65 apples how many apples did he pack

11 A vegetable seller had 79885 vegetables He has to pack them in boxes with each box containing 425 apples Find the number of boxes required to pack vegetables

12 Machine A can produce 6500 biscuits in a day , which is 240 fewer biscuits than what machine B can produce in a day Now 20 biscuits are placed in a pack if both machines A and B are used how many packs of biscuits will be there after 7 days ?

CHAPTER EIGHT

MISCELLANEOUS

1. Calcul;ate 8x4/2

2 Calculate 2/4 + 1/6

3 Count back in from 45 in 8s

4 Complete the sentence using the correct word

In the number 15.862 the 2 represents two ___

5. Write a decimal number on each answer line to make each statement correct

443 hundredths

84 tenths and 2 thousandths

7 ones 2 hundredths and 5 thousandths

7+0.7+0.03

6 Convert into decimals

a.5/20

b.2/5

c.8/10

d.1/4

e.1/2

f.17/50

g.4/5

h.75/1000

i.5/10

j 16/50

7.Add fractions

3/8 + 4/8

2/4 + 1/4

8. On Monday Eve climbs 40 lengths of the tree

On Tuesday she climbs 5o percent more lengths than on Monday

On Wednesday she climbs 50 percent fewer lengths than on Tuesday
Calculate the **Total** number of lengths she climbs on the three days

12

www.ingramcontent.com/pod-product-compliance
Lightning Source LLC
Chambersburg PA
CBHW040544160726
48005CB00040B/1801